Be Still, My Dear Gay Heart

Ron Rebholz

authorHOUSE®

AuthorHouse™
1663 Liberty Drive, Suite 200
Bloomington, IN 47403
www.authorhouse.com
Phone: 1-800-839-8640

First published by AuthorHouse 3/9/2009

ISBN: 978-1-4343-4588-2 (sc)

Printed in the United States of America
Bloomington, Indiana

This book is printed on acid-free paper.

I dedicate this book to my friends and lovers.

St. Louis

In 1932, when I was born, my father was a blue collar worker in the basement of the First National Bank of St. Louis, pouring money into a coin-counting machine, making stacks of bills, and then recording the sums in a book of accounts. He had taken a job there in 1919, at the age of nineteen, having lost a job at another bank, and, with only a high school education, was afraid to look for something better when the Depression hit. He was an intelligent man who loved to read, and was gradually going blind because he read at the kitchen table in the bad overhead light. He was in many ways my hero. A deep admirer of FDR, he tried in 1946, along with four other workers, to organize a union of blue collar workers at the bank. The bank spent a million dollars fighting the potential union, and, on the night before the election, invited all of the workers to a cocktail party and dinner in St. Louis's swankiest hotel, where all the vice presidents promised the workers that they would get everything the union stood for without having to pay dues. The next day they voted down the union by a 5 to 1 margin, and my father never got another raise, retiring at sixty-five making $400 a month.

My mother's parents objected to her fiancée because he was Catholic and they were fundamentalist Lutherans. So my future mother and father had to meet secretly on street corners to court. Her parents never forgave her for her marriage, and they never invited my father for a meal. After I was born they invited my mother and me for the occasional meal. My grandfather, who was a paper hanger, would hang paper in my parents' house but not each lunch with my mother. I genuinely disliked both my grandmother and grandfather, the more I knew them. It was not unusual for my grandfather, if he came home before his supper was ready, to sweep all the pots and pans off the stove and make my grandmother pick them up.

My parents had bought a little house before they got married, but their plan to move there changed right after their wedding. My mother, who worked as a wrapper in a big department store, was run over by a car when she was getting off a bus and spent the next ten months in the hospital with a compound fracture of her right leg. Without her income, my father could not afford the mortgage, so he sold the house and moved in with his mother.

My paternal grandmother ran a boarding house, renting out all of the rooms except for her bedroom upstairs, and feeding six people. It was a handsome house, two stories of brick on a stone foundation, in the predominantly German section of St. Louis. When my mother got out of the hospital, my grandmother gave my parents two rooms downstairs as a living room and a bedroom and now fed them and four boarders in the big kitchen with a wood burning stove. There was no place for me to sleep, so I spent the first thirteen years of my life sleeping with my grandmother. Then, in her infinite German wisdom, she windowed in the back porch for my bed, a sofa, and the newly acquired TV set. I loved my grandmother very much and was devastated by her death when I was seventeen. When I was very young, I was closer to my father than my mother, and I remember fondly the walks we took each night after he got home from work, hand in hand, to the railroad tracks two blocks away to watch the six o'clock special on its way from Chicago to New Orleans and dreamed of someday getting on that train.

We could in fact afford only the simplest driving trips. My father loved Chicago. We would be setting out for a picnic in the local park and suddenly the car was on its way up Highway 66 to Chicago. My mother, who had on a light dress for a picnic, was freezing as we checked into the cheapest hotel on Lake Michigan. I had a great time, with my father taking me to the Field Museum of Natural History, the Adler Planetarium, and the top of the Wrigley Building. He also wanted to stop in the burlesque houses on State Street, but my freezing mother resisted.

The other trip that sticks in my memory was a radical departure from the Chicago destination. My mother wanted to see New Orleans, and my father was interested, so we set out south. Because I was fifteen years old and had a learner's permit, my father decided to let me do some of the driving while he napped in the back seat. My mother insisted that I turn off the radio lest I be distracted from the road, but it was the radio that kept me awake. When the road curved to the left, I was sound asleep and continued straight ahead off the road. My father woke up yelling, "You're going to kill us, Ronald, you're going to kill us." My mother screamed as I braked on some slick, high grass and slowly slid to the edge of a muddy creak and toppled over. There we were, almost upside down in the mud. Cars and trucks stopped on the highway, and some people righted the car sufficiently to drag us out. A kind soul went into the nearest town, Grenada, to fetch a tow truck, which pulled the car out of the creak and set us on our way. The only damage was a tiny scratch on one fender. The mud had saved us, as had the absence of a cliff.

Some experiences made a lasting impression on me. I think of one in particular: my father's attempt to teach me how to swim. My mother and he took me to the local public pool. He took me into the pool while my mother sat in a chair next to the pool and watched. She was terrified of water because a boy had dunked her when she was a young girl and ignored her attempts to come up for air. Someone stepped on her and, realizing there was a body at the bottom of the pool, called for a life guard. So, sitting anxiously by the pool as my father was trying to get me to float, she started to scream: "Al, he's going to drown, he's going to drown." Her fear of water was transferred to me, and, despite many attempts at lessons, I to this day cannot swim and am almost deadly afraid of water.

I knew I was gay from the first moment I was conscious of sexuality. In grade school I was in love with a boy from the Ozarks, named Bobby Mackie. I biked miles to get to his house and play pick-up baseball in a park nearby. I didn't tell him I loved him, but it must have showed to others because one day, as were going outside for recess, a group of boys forced us to kiss. It didn't take much for me to comply, and I liked to think Bobby enjoyed it. We didn't discuss the kiss on my subsequent visits, but I wanted desperately to repeat it.

My first job as a kid was selling soda at Sportsman Park for Cardinal and Browns games in the summer. When I was thirteen I got a job as an usher at the park, having to join a company union to be eligible to work for $3 a game. I met another usher, Dan, a couple of years older than me. I adored him and his blue-grey sweater that is still fixed in my memory. We would usher as close together as possible and hang out briefly after the game. But Dan got a better job, and I ushered throughout most of my high school years, adding basketball, hockey games, and professional wrestling to my schedule. One summer I also worked in an ice house, checking the delivery drivers as they set out and making sure they didn't steal any money when they checked back in. I didn't like or admire any of these men, but the pay was decent.

I was always a favorite of the nuns who taught in our grammar school—much to the disgust of the other boys who called me a "suck-up." I arrived early to help carry the nuns' suitcases of class material from the convent to the school. I paid attention in class and volunteered to answer questions. At times my behavior was self-protective: one nun, a Sister Lillian, would punish a student, usually a boy, by grabbing his ears and beating the back of his head against the iron radiators that lined the walls of the classroom. We were so terrified of her that no one told the parents or the principal. At other times I actually loved my nuns. When I was in eighth grade the teacher, who was also the principal, chose me to sing "Silent Night" in the procession before midnight mass. Unfortunately my voice broke on the high note, and I almost dropped my candle.

I was a boy scout when I was in grade school, and our troop leader, no more than seventeen years old, was called Doc, because we met in a room above the office of his father, a doctor in South St. Louis. One evening it got into the head of five of the older boys to pants Doc, and when he was naked I was told to jack him off. I did so with pleasure, and we were all excited when he sent streams of cum all over his body from his face down. The other boys released him and jacked off on his body. That was the first time I had seen cum.

I was always in love with one or two of my classmates in grade school and high school, but of course I didn't tell them. I was something of a star on our high school debate team and in ex tempore speech contests. One night my debate partner invited me over to the house of his aunt, who was on vacation, to work on our case. After dinner served by a maid, John suggested we play strip poker before going to bed. I was astonished by the size of John's cock when it was hard, at least nine or ten inches, and he was small boy. Then he suggested we play "capture the fort," and we grabbed each other's cocks before wrestling away. I finally got too frustrated with this game, so I sat on top of him and started massaging his cock. He came in a flurry of cum, and I jacked off on top of him. Again, we never discussed or repeated the incident.

A break through moment came in the senior year of high school. A priest for whom I had great admiration became the personal confessor of seniors who wished to confess face to face. I literally seduced the priest, so when I read stories of child abuse by the clergy I always wonder to what degree the child, in this case a young man of seventeen, is responsible. I was a thoughtless person, asking the priest to hear my confession after we had made love. I never knew how he coped with our affair or to whom he made his confessions.

I almost did not go to college because my parents could not afford tuition and certainly not room and board if I went to the University of Missouri in Columbia Missouri. But the priest whom I had seduced, who was head of the alumni association, and for whom I worked one summer, raised the money from alums to get me a scholarship to St. Louis University, the local Jesuit school. I was virtually a rent boy, and I didn't have the good grace to continue to see my patron, as I tried, unsuccessfully, to seduce the priest who taught first-year English, Shakespeare, and Renaissance literature at the university. But the example of my high school priest led me to be a teacher, and my university professor showed me what I would eventually want to teach.

In the summer of my sophomore year I went to Corpus Christi, Texas, at the invitation of a friend whom I was in love with. I was disappointed to learn that, while I could stay with his parents, he himself was spending the summer elsewhere. His folks got me a job painting pipes in an oil field, which was a dreadfully hot task, especially when I was sitting on top of a pipe or lying underneath one that almost touched my face. I had three work mates, one of whom was very cute but unfortunately straight. They decided to take advantage of his car and drive to Monterrey after work on a Friday and spend the weekend getting to know something about Mexico. I found the bull fights fascinating, although I always, silently, rooted for the bull. I did not find fascinating the whorehouse we went to. I was actually disgusted by the women who insisted on sitting on my lap as I plied them with beer. I would much have preferred to have one of my mates on my lap, but that was not approved in Mexican culture, and probably still isn't, at least not in public places.

In the spring break of my junior year I went to Minneapolis with a friend to apply for a summer job as a bus boy at Glacier National Park. We slept in the same bed in his house, and during the night I felt him fondling my limp cock. I grabbed his hand and held it on my cock until I had an erection, and then I took his hard cock from his pajama bottom. I leaned over and kissed him, and thanked him for doing something I was too frightened to do. I took off his and my pajamas, and we had passionate sex. This time we continued to have sex in his dorm room throughout the rest of the spring, experimenting with sucking. But the school year came to an end, and we went to different hotels in Glacier, cursed with roommates that deprived us of privacy, and our lovely affair came to an end.

In my senior year in college I told one of my friends that I loved him, and he said he would prove that he loved me just as much with a kiss. The kiss was delicious, and it lasted while we undid each other's zippers and grabbed each other's cocks inside our underwear. Then he suggested that we do it the right way in a park next to my car. In the deep darkness of the park we undressed each other and came together in a rush of excitement. We invented occasions, like a speech tournament in a neighboring town in Illinois, to escape the scrutiny of our parents and make love in a real bed. But I went off to graduate school at Stanford in 1953, and he went to a law school in St. Louis.

These were was the only sexual experiences I had until I was drafted in the army in 1954. I needed, of course, a cover, so I took one girl to dances in high school and a different one in university. My kisses at the door were just little pecks. Jane, my high school "date," finally asked me in our senior year if I had any serious intentions about our relationship. I told here I didn't, but I was too cowardly to tell her why. I'm glad to say that she married happily, as did Shirley, the woman I went with in university, although our breakup was much more sticky. After her parents invited me and my parents to visit them in Oklahoma City, I had to make a quick separation because I had let the "affair" carry on too long.

I was always a good student, and had scholarships to a Catholic grade school, a Jesuit high school, St. Louis University, Stanford University, and Oxford. The same priest whom I seduced in high school awakened my interest in English literature with his own version of a Norton survey from *Beowulf* to the twentieth century. My interest was confirmed and focused by the priest at the university who taught me in Shakespeare and Renaissance courses.

I worked on the newspaper at the university, and when told to write a story about Korea I had to ask where it was. I worked for the radio station as a kind of disk jockey and acted in radio drama. I was a public address announcer for the university basketball team's games, and thought about making a career in radio. My father wanted me to become a lawyer because the law paid well, and, with my training in debate, I believe I could have been an effective trial lawyer. But I decided finally to become a teacher of literature like the two great teachers who had inspired my interest in literature.

Stanford and Long Beach, California

With that intention I began graduate work in English at Stanford in the autumn of 1954, supported by a Danforth Fellowship and a Woodrow Wilson fellowship. It was an academically eventful year, the highlights of which were three courses from the eminent critic, Yvor Winters. Graduate students' were housed in a reclaimed army hospital barracks in Menlo Park, about three miles north of the campus, and we had to hitch hike to campus. My roommate was Joe Maltby, a gifted young student who at that time was primarily interested in Restoration comedy. I tried to seduce Joe with protestations of love, but he said he was not interested in that kind of love and sex. He let me down gently, and we became good friends.

Joe introduced me to the music of Gustav Mahler. Whenever a new recording of a Mahler symphony was released Joe played it many times before he and his brother in Long Beach had lengthy phone conversations about the symphony and the quality of the recording. I could only avoid learning something about Mahler if I left our room, and I was taken by the music and became a Mahler fan to this day. Joe also introduced me to hard liquor. Every Friday night, we hitched a ride with a friend who had a car and drove to a warm French bar and restaurant south of the campus. L'Omelette's served marvelous gin martinis, now my favorite drink.

Joe also invited me to his home in Long Beach for the Christmas and New Year break. There I met his brother who had set up a kind of altar in one bedroom, with a table covered by an elegant cloth and a record player in the center, where in darkness and silence we listened to all of Mahler's symphonies for which there were recordings and all of the symphonies of Sibelius. On New Year's eve Joe threw a small party for me, his brother, and some local friends. He served screwdrivers which I had never tasted before. I kept asking him to put some liquor in my drink because all I could taste was orange juice. As the new year was rung in on the radio he opened a bottle of champagne, and I had a big glass. When Joe suggested that we take a walk down to the beach, the party went out the front door to the right, and I walked off to the left. The air hit my alcohol soaked head, and I walked the streets of Long Beach until four in the morning, vomiting at every corner. I swore the next day I would never drink another screwdriver, and I haven't.

I had tried for a Rhodes Scholarship in my senior year at St. Louis University and did not get one. I decided to apply again from Stanford, but when the time for the interview on December 8 approached, I decided I couldn't afford the trip to St. Louis, and I informed the Rhodes secretary that I was withdrawing. He phoned William Danforth and told him that I had a good chance this time, and Mr. Danforth phoned me. You can imagine my surprise when I walked down the hall to the telephone and heard his gruff voice tell me that there was a plane ticket for me at the airport and that I better get on that plane. This time I did succeed at the local level and shortly thereafter at the district level in Des Moines, Iowa.

Camp Chafee, Arkansas and Fort Lewis, Washington

I had every intention of entering Oxford in the autumn of 1954 and was home visting my parents in the summer when I got the notice that I was to report for military duty at Camp Chafee outside of Fort Smith, Arkansas in September, a place that we came to call the armpit of the nation. I was heart sick. I wrote my Senators and Congressman and phoned the American Secretary, Courtney Smith, begging them to get me out of the army so I could go to Oxford. Smith said that scholars had been very well treated by the draft boards and that I should not spoil the situation for other candidates by resisting my board. So I went into the army. In retrospect, I am glad that I did. I had had too many consecutive years of school and was getting stale. Two years in the army made school seem fresh again.

I could not have predicted that possibility during basic training in the armpit. I hated the obstacle courses. My weak arms did not get me up and over walls ("Walk around it, buddy" was a constant refrain) or up and down ropes. I dreaded crawling at night toward a bank of machine guns with live ammunition shooting just above our heads, flares dancing above us. I loathed the long marches with a heavy pack toward nowhere, culminating in a field where we slept on the ground and tried to cover ourselves with the half of a tent that each of us carried. Once we ended up in a kind of valley with the land sloping towards a central field. I and another nice man attached our two tent-halves, pitched the tent, pinned it to the ground, and dug a trench around it in case it rained. It did rain and the wind blew. Soon we found ourselves sleeping on a pool of water, our trench flooded. But at least our tent remained up; many around us had their tents blown over, and they were sleeping on the drenched ground and in the relentless rain. The only exercise I mildly enjoyed was shooting the M1 rifle, but keeping it clean was an endless task. All of this agony was punctuated by the threat—"We are going to ship your asses to Korea"—if we made mistakes or showed discontent.

After eight weeks of military basic, each of us was assigned to "advanced" basic for training in what would become our specialty. I was fortunate to have taken typing in high school, so I was a star in clerk typist basic, winning a medal for the fastest typist in our class. But I never wanted to see the armpit again.

After basic training, I was shipped to Japan, although I came very close to going to Korea. At Fort Lewis, Washington, where all men going to the Far East were given their assignments, my friends from Arkansas and I banded together to try to get into the small assignment building at the same time. It took days of running to the door after the morning formation before we finally made it. But it sounded like a Korea day, with cooks, mechanics, riflemen, and clerk typists all going to Korea. Just as we reached the desk there was a shout—"Five clerk typists for Japan"—and we were saved.

Sendai and Tokyo, Japan

After a turbulent journey in which everyone got sea-sick, we docked in Yokohama. I was stationed for the first six months in Sendai, a northern city. Being "stationed" there is a slight euphemism. Trained as a clerk typist, I was the junior member of a small group— a warrant officer, a master sergeant, two sergeants, and me—called the Personnel Management Inspection Team whose home was the headquarters of the First Cavalry Division but whose job was to travel to all the places where the division was based in all three major islands. Our duty was to inspect all personnel records to insure they were properly maintained and to guarantee that men were assigned to jobs for which they had been trained in civilian life and the army. When we found someone trained as a mechanic being a cook and someone trained as a cook working in the motor pool, my job was to type a recommendation, which went all the way up to the commanding general of the division and all the way back to the unit in question, that the jobs of the cook and mechanic be switched. When we went back six months later and the jobs had not been switched, I typed a reprimand of the responsible officer that again traveled all the way up and down. When we went back again six months later, the officer, the cook, and the mechanic had all returned to the States. We did not achieve a single reassignment in the eighteen months I was in Japan. We did improve the maintenance of the records and, because our chief was a warrant officer who was more interested in seeing Japan than in looking at personnel records, we had the luxury of three-day weekends for travel, and I did a lot of traveling.

After the first year, division headquarters were moved from Sendai to Tokyo, and that became our home base. The transfer was a comedy of errors, with all the vehicles we were driving down a rough road running out of gas about an hour out of Tokyo. The commanding officer, who had assured us, after being questioned, that we had enough gas for the journey, snuck into Tokyo and brought back cans of gas that he used to fill up our trucks and jeeps, and we limped into the new headquarters.

An advance team had prepared our barracks, and I found myself in a bed next to a gorgeous redhead who had asked that I be bunked there, having heard from a sergeant in the advance team that he might like me. Jerry had made my bed and suggested that we attend a sermon of a missionary in downtown Tokyo. Except for the prospect of being with Jerry, I had no appetite for a sermon, but I went along on an army bus that took us to the church, my head lolling on his shoulder as I kept falling asleep. We became fast friends.

When I was not on the road, we went to movies together and frequented teahouses and bars. One Sunday afternoon, we went to see a 1955 movie, *Love is a Many-Splendored Thing*, whose only legacy is a song with that title. It was a very romantic film, and about half way through it I felt Jerry's knee pressing against mine. I returned the pressure, and we sat that way through the rest of the movie. We were a little flustered, as we went back to the barracks, not sure how to interpret the touches.

Our team was shipped to Kyoto the next day, and two days later I received a letter from Jerry (the army postal service was very efficient). In it he said how much he enjoyed my company and wished that I weren't traveling so much. It came as close to a declaration of love as it could without quite crossing the line. I immediately replied that I shared his feelings and looked forward to seeing him soon. He later told me that he had to hide himself in a toilet to avoid showing his excitement as he read my letter.

When I returned to headquarters, we could hardly avoid kissing. We had the good fortune that the sergeant who had set us up was going out of town and said we could use his room instead of sleeping in the barracks. Dressed only in our under shorts and T-shirts, we sat on the sergeant's bed. I said I couldn't be in his presence without getting an erection, and he said it was true for him as well. We kissed and stood together looking out a big window on the lights of the city. We embraced, our erections meeting each other. I took off his T-shirt, and he took off mine. I then knelt down and pulled his shorts down and around his beautiful cock. He then did the same for me. Jerry said it wasn't prudent to come on the floor, so I fetched a towel and spread it on top of the sheets. We lay next to each other, and the intensity of our kiss made us both come. It was the most wonderful moment of my life thus far.

We could not get enough of each other. When I was stationed somewhere near Tokyo, I would rent a room in a hotel for the weekend, and Jerry would join me, usually arriving by ferry or train. When I was stationed in Tokyo, we would get a room in a rest and recreation hotel the army had bought or in a Japanese hotel. During the week we made love in the doorway of the barracks or in the toilet, taking ridiculous risks. Those were blissful days.

When we returned to the States, our homes were close enough together that we could drive to meet at his place or mine. Jerry always insisted, both in the army and after we were discharged, that we go to confession after we had made love, knowing full well that we had no intention of amending our lives. At least I did; Jerry may have been fooling himself. Once in St. Louis the priest demanded that I promise not to see Jerry again. I said I wouldn't and stormed out of the confessional.

Looming over us was the knowledge that I was going to be leaving soon to take up my Rhodes Scholarship in Oxford. Jerry begged me not to go, arguing that we could set up a household and live together forever. I did not want to give up the scholarship, so we parted in September of 1956. Jerry immediately married a woman to whom he was not attracted and had five kids by her. He ultimately settled with a very nice man in Tucson, but he died of cancer in 2004.

Oxford, England

I first met Dick Sylvester at a tea party at Swarthmore College for Rhodes Scholars about to sail to England. I had recently been released from the U.S. army as a specialist 2nd class, the equivalent of a corporal. Courtney Smith, the president of Swarthmore and the American Secretary of the Rhodes Trust, escorted me across the room, saying "I'm sure you would like to meet Richard Sylvester. He's a graduate of West Point, and he's also going to be a student at Worcester College." "I suppose I'll have to address you as Lieutenant Sylvester," I snapped. We instantly disliked each other, and I don't believe we said more than a few words on the Flandre in the five-day journey to Southampton.

We were met at the dock by Bill Williams, the Warden of Rhodes House, who got us on board a train to Oxford, where we were met by a bus and taken to Rhodes House for hot dogs and wine, the Warden's way of working the transition from the U.S. to England. At about 10:00 p.m. the Warden announced that taxis were out front to take us and our luggage to our colleges. I couldn't avoid Dick Sylvester then, although we didn't speak to each other in the taxi.

When we arrived at Worcester, the quadrangle was sunk in a thick fog. The porter informed us that there was another American in residence, but that the other students would not be arriving for a couple of days. Dick and I were thrust together by a shared terror. I asked if I might accompany him and the porter to his rooms in the 18th century building, and he asked if he could accompany me and the porter to my rooms in the 13th century pump quad. I had spirited a little bottle of whiskey from the boat, and I offered Dick a drink. From that moment we became the best of friends.

When Dick switched his degree program from philosophy, politics, and economics to English language and literature, we had the same tutors: Christopher Tolkien for the history of the English language, *Beowulf*, and Chaucer, and ancient Colonel Wilkinson for the rest of English literature through Byron, which was when literature to be studied academically stopped in 1956. Tolkien was a miserable man. Growing up in the shadow of his famous father, he was so depressed that he almost failed his exams in Oxford. We learned nothing from him. He has since made a small fortune, editing a previously unknown work of his father, a fortune that probably had something to do with his being made a fellow of New College. Wilkinson was a collector of rare books, who thought that we would understand the poems of John Donne if he put a copy of the first edition in our lap. But he was a kind man who was particularly fond of Americans, so Dick and I had a few invitations to visit him during break, at his "house on the mud across from the Isle of Wight." We did learn that he had been in the army in the first world war and that he was in charge of the Oxford equivalent of the ROTC during the second. We speculated that he had his job because he and the head of the college, J.C. Masterman, had been lovers, but theirs was a generation we could not fathom.

We had many good times in our first year. Because Dick had access to the PX on a base not far from Oxford, he hosted some wonderful parties. We laughed at the abominable mutton and broad beans that was standard fare in the college hall, and cracked jokes about the incompetence of our tutors. I especially remember meeting Laurence OIivier and Vivian Leigh at the college. Every year Oxford confers honorary degrees on famous people, a ceremony followed by a garden party for the honorees. That year it was Worcester College's turn to host the party. We were forbidden to attend the party, but Dick, I and two other intrepid students put on our gowns and, armed with cameras, crashed the party, only to be told that Olivier and Leigh had just left. We dashed to the front of the college, and there was Leigh leaning against the fence waiting for Olivier to fetch the chauffeur and the car. She said that they had just returned from Yugoslavia where they had performed the leads in Shakespeare's dreadful revenge tragedy, *Titus Andronicus.* and that she had been bitten by a snake there. We invited her for a drink, and when Olivier returned and announced that the chauffeur was stuck in traffic and would only be a few moments, Leigh said that she had accepted an invitation for a drink from "these nice boys." Olivier was furious. "Vivien, you know we must get you to the doctor for an injection to deal with that snake bite." "Oh Larry, a glass of gin will be much better for me than a stupid doctor's injection." She prevailed, and we escorted them back to one of our friend's room. She sat on a sofa, downing two large glasses of gin while he leaned against a bureau and looked daggers at her. She wondered if she was better in *Gone With The Wind* or *A Streetcar Named Desire.* We asked him what it was like to play Titus, and he said it was like chewing straw. He almost had to drag her out when she was asking for a third gin. It was quite clear that this marriage was on the rocks, as indeed it was.

Our other brush with greatness that year came with the invitation from the Lovelace Society, Worcester's literary club, to W. H. Auden, who was Oxford's professor of poetry at that time, for drinks, dinner, and a talk. Auden, whose face looked ravaged by time, got extremely drunk and said he didn't want to talk about poetry but just gossip. We helped him get back to All Souls' College where the poetry professor is traditionally lodged.

I acted in the college play that year. Worcester is the only college with a lake on its grounds, and the play, *Toad of Toad Hall*, was set by the lake. I was cast as Chief Weasel because the director said my accent reminded him of a Chicago gangster's. I had the opportunity to push Toad into the lake.

Dick and I often took the 5:00 p.m. fast train to London on a Friday, booked ourselves into a B&B near Russell Square, and went to as many plays as we could on Saturday and Sunday evening before returning to Oxford on what we called the cattle train at 11:00 p.m., arriving at Oxford at 2:00 a.m. We went skiing in Austria during the winter break and toured the east coast of Spain in the spring break.

We also fell in love, I with Dick and he with Mike Hammond, a Rhodes scholar in Balliol College whom Dick had met at a party. Both loves were unreciprocated.

In the long summer vacation I first went on a car trip with Richard Aldridge, a witty and talented poet at Worcester, and Charles, a friend of his from a different college who had a car. We drove to Harwich in Essex, caught an overnight ferry to Ebjerg in Denmark, and drove to Copenhagen where we booked a room and went to the Tivoli Gardens for dinner. All three of us ordered lobster. This was my first encounter with that impossible shell fish, and I broke the table up when I dipped my first piece of lobster in the finger bowl.We then drove to Sweden and then to northern Germany. Charles hated Germany and the Germans because he and his mother had almost been killed by a bomb that destroyed the house of their neighbor and friend two houses down. I broke off from the trip at that point and took the train to Limburg an-der-Lahn where I spent a week with the relatives of some German friends from St. Louis

I then met up with Dick at Heidelberg which I reached by train. Dick, who had gone to Bayreuth to take in Wagner's *Ring*, had a VW by this time, and we drove it across the Alps to Venice and then to Verona to see *Carmen* in the Roman amphitheatre.

Just as the conductor began the overture, a mighty storm blew down the city of Seville and the last opera of the year was cancelled. Disconsolate, we went to bed, and that night, because for the first time we were sleeping in the same bed, I made my move, playing with Dick's cock until it got hard but not waking him up.

The next morning there were signs on every lamppost announcing a "performance extraordinaire" of *La Boheme* with Renata Tibaldi in the lead role. I thought it would be an auspicious moment to tell Dick, who was in a good mood about the opera, that I had played with him because I was in love with him. So over breakfast I blurted out the truth. I could not have been more wrong about the timing as well as his willingness to hear my declaration of love. The chilly silence between us for the rest of the day reminded me of those days aboard the Flandre. We ate dinner in silence and attended the opera without comment. It seemed that I had ruined the summer vacation for him.

We cut short our trip in Italy and drove back to Paris. There an extraordinary thing happened. Dick got out of his bed and came into mine, asking that I do with him what I did with other men. I undressed him, kissed him, and jacked him off, not daring to go farther than the simplest sexual act. He confessed that he had once had sex with another student when he was on a summer exercise in artillery, but he insisted that he didn't want to discuss what we had done and definitely not repeat it. Back in Oxford, we had to share a rented room because the college was not yet open, and Dick punished me by making me listen to the *Ring* on the radio in a London performance.

My second year was a very unhappy one. I was still living in college, but Dick had moved to a house in north Oxford ("digs," as they were called by the Brits) shared by Mike Hammond and three other Rhodes Scholars. I thought I was in love with Charles who was living in digs, and began a sexual affair with him. But then I realized that I was in love with a student in my own college who did not reciprocate. When I told Charles that I wasn't in love with him after all, he attempted to cut his wrist and then downed a bottle of sleeping pills. He and Dick had been taking instructions from a brilliant priest at the Newman Society, he to become closer to me and Dick to become closer to Mike Hammond. I raced to the Newman house to fetch the priest in the hope that he would be able to talk Charles into living. I then knocked on the door of the local doctor who committed him to the hospital where they pumped his stomach. I had caused Charles to have a nervous breakdown, the worst thing I had done in my life after the seduction and subsequent neglect of the priest in high school.

One of the oarsmen in the college boat drowned. Dick was in the boat as it capsized and saw his mate drawn through the weir. His body was found much later in the Thames in London.

As president of the Lovelace Society it was my responsibility to canvass the members about whom they would like to invite for the annual dinner and then let the Provost make the choice because he would spend the night in the Provost's lodge if he was not from Oxford. I told Masterman that our first choice was Laurence Olivier, and he said Larry would be too busy in London to come up for the event. Our second choice was Paul Robeson, the great Black bass and member of the communist party in the U.S. who was playing Othello in London. The Provost said that he didn't think Robeson would give us quite what we were looking for. I wasn't sure if his objection was his race or his politics. Our third choice was William Empson, the great literary critic who could come from London where he was living at that time. The Provost asked me to take a biographical dictionary from his shelf and read its account of Empson. I got to the fact that he was educated at Winchester and Magdalen College, Cambridge, and the Provost said he would be just fine. He turned out to be so eccentric that we could scarcely speak to him. The Provost had done his homework and asked him at dinner about his life as a journalist in the Far East. Empson rolled his eyes up so that only the whites showed and said it was interesting. I asked him where he came up with the topic for his famous book, *Seven Types of Ambiguity*, and he said if I had read the book it was obvious. The next day, after I had seen Empson to a cab for the train station, the Provost stopped me in the quadrangle and said that that man was the strangest product of Winchester and Magdalen that he had ever encountered. The event was a bust.

I asked a woman friend to go with me on a skiing trip in Austria, thinking that I would part with my gay past and become a straight man. But when we got to the inn and the innkeeper called out my name and hers to show us to our room, I panicked. I threw myself on the bed and said that I couldn't have sex with her, this time telling her the truth. The next day she fell when she was getting on the chair and hurt her hip, so now she was not going to make love or go skiing. That year I had an uncanny knack of spoiling people's lives.

I sat the schools, Oxford's way of referring to the final exams, at the end of my second year, and stayed on to do a D.Phil. Schools at Oxford were very difficult: nine three-hour papers stretched across a week, two per day. One day I overslept and had only two hours to attempt the paper. Those who were on the margin of a first class and second class degree were summoned for an oral exam, called a *viva voce*, and that was my fate. The paper I had only two hours to complete had caught the examiners' eyes, and I was quizzed on it for about forty minutes. I was surprised and delighted to receive a first.

My life from 1958 to 1961 was pretty dreary. For two years I was living in digs with Charles and going to lots of movies to keep him entertained and distracted from killing himself. I had a hard time finding a subject for my dissertation, and my supervisor, Dame Helen Gardner, an eminent critic of Renaissance literature and T. S. Eliot, was of no use until I had written something, which she then tore apart. She used me as a manual laborer to reorganize her library in her house outside Oxford. I took a job at Stanford in 1961 without a completed dissertation, a huge mistake, but I had exhausted all of my scholarships and needed to make a living. I had to go back to England in the summer of 1963 to finish my research, mainly at the British Museum, and in 1964 to be examined on the end result. The expense was great, as was the stress, because I was developing seven new courses and living on a salary frozen at $6000 until I finished.

There were a few good moment in those days in London. Once I had a small flat around the corner from a TV store, and I spent a lot of time looking at cricket matches through the window. I read all three volumes of the *Lord of the Ring* without stopping to sleep. Best of all, I met on the deck of the Greek Liner from New York to London a cute young scholar from Northwestern who was going to London for research. We discovered that we were both gay, and he spent a good deal of time in my flat teaching me how to be fucked. I corresponded with him, and I once visited him in Chicago when I was going to a convention of the Modern Language Association.

I finally completed my degree in 1964, three years after I had taken the job at Stanford. Because he had switched subjects, Dick took his exams at the end of his third year. All of the time after that summer vacation we were cordial, and I resigned myself to our simply becoming friends. But my life was full of surprises. In the summer after my first year at Stanford, I was house-sitting for a distinguished English scholar, R. F. Jones, in a lovely house just off the Stanford campus. My parents had paid me a visit early in the summer, and I was working on my dissertation when I got a letter from Dick asking if he could visit me. I mailed back the directions, and he arrived at the Jones's house dejected. He had just returned from Hawaii where he had proposed to the daughter of a general and had been turned down. His military career also wasn't satisfying him. It seemed clear to me that he was drawing on the residue of our friendship to find some temporary consolation, and that he was allowing himself to be vulnerable to making love, which we did rather heatedly and frequently in the week that he stayed at Stanford before going back to Fort Sill and the artillery.

We corresponded frequently after that visit, and I learned that Dick had got a position at West Point teaching English, that he had decided to resign his commission, only to be put on orders to Korea as punishment, and that he had used a contact with a former Rhodes Scholar in the State Department to escape the clutches of the army. He entered the Ph.D. program at Harvard's Russian department, having studied the language at the University of Minnesota while he was waiting to depart on his scholarship to Oxford. He told me that he loved the language, and that he was determined to get the degree despite the unhelpful and unfriendly faculty members in the department, reminiscent of those tutors at Oxford.

Because his dissertation required some research in the archives of the Hoover Institution at Stanford, he asked if he could stay with me for about six weeks in the summer. I was living in a one-room guesthouse on top of a beautiful hill, with an apricot orchard in the back yard—an ideal place to work and to make love. I believed that Dck had finally fallen in love with me.

Cambridge, Massachusetts

Those six weeks were so blissful that I decided to spend my sabbatical year, beginning in the autumn of 1967, with Dick, revising my dissertation into a book at the Houghton Library in Cambridge, if he would have me, and he was pleased to put me up in his tiny garret apartment near the park in the center of Cambridge. Those also were generally happy days, tarnished only by the occasional visits of women that his friends in Washington were trying to fix him up with. When he spent a weekend with one of them, I flew into a jealous rage that even I didn't know I was capable of, and he apologized. We worked hard but made time for play. We became quite good cooks and connoisseurs of wine. I still have the scrapbook of wine labels that we carefully removed from the bottles and glossed with our judgments of the wine.

We had a wonderful routine for our Sundays when no work was allowed. We got up late, read the papers, put a bottle of white wine in the refrigerator, and started the preparations of a supper that would be very easy to finish. We then smoked some grass and, on fine days, lounged on the ground in the park listening to the rock concerts that were a Cambridge ritual, or, on days that were wet, went to museums in Boston. When we came home, we finished the supper and ate it with the chilled wine. We then made love and went to sleep.

Harlaxton Manor, Grantham, England

At the end of the summer, Dick went to Leningrad as an exchange student and I drove back to Stanford and boarded a plane to London, a train to Grantham, and a taxi to Harlaxton Manor, a Victorian pseudo-Gothic pile in the middle of nowhere and the first of Stanford's campuses in Britain. I joined another Stanford faculty member and an English lecturer to make up the teaching staff. My job was to lecture to the twenty some students on Shakespeare and conduct a seminar on Renaissance literature with about half of them. *Time* once described Grantham as the most boring city in the world, and the Stanford administration planned to console the students for putting up with this city and the cold, Victorian building with a field trip to Paris in late October near the end of the autumn term.

Dick sent me a few postcards describing how beautiful Leningrad was and encouraging me to come for a visit. So, instead of going to Paris, I booked a flight on Aeroflot from London to Leningrad on October 27, 1968, a journey that led to the most frightening events of my life, scarring my consciousness and my memory to this day.

Leningrad and Tallinn

Dick met me at the airport with a briefcase full of bread, butter, caviar, vodka, and grass. A 30-minute taxi ride took us to the Astoria hotel, not a place I had chosen but a hotel where the government housed foreign visitors. In the cab Dick told me that he had made arrangements, after six nights in Leningrad, for a three-day trip to Tallinn, the capital of Estonia and reputedly a very beautiful 13th century city.

In the hall of every Russian hotel sits a little old lady in black who issues the key to your room when you come in and collects it when you leave. Our feast lasted well beyond midnight when the drawbridge over the river Neva is lifted, cutting Dick off from the student residence across the river, so the lady in black did not get the key. We didn't mind because it gave us the opportunity to end weeks of frustration and make love. The next morning we gave the key to the lady in black and had a breakfast in the hotel dining room that included several ounces of caviar. We then made the first of several trips to the Hermitage.

The remainder of the week followed the same pattern. Dick spent the night in the hotel, and we toured Leningrad and its surrounds in the day, including Dick's student residence to pick up a toothbrush, and attended ballets, operas, and concerts during the evening. One day we took a train to Pushkin to visit acquaintances Dick had met, a woman who was an engineer for the Pushkin water company and her ancient mother, living together in a small apartment with a screen dividing the room. They treated us to a lovely ham and salad lunch, while the mother reminisced about Czarist Russia and the revolution and the daughter told us how lucky they felt finally to have a room to themselves. On another day we visited the room of Joseph Brodsky off a coal black kitchen in an old house. Dick had made his acquaintance, and Brodsky, who was translating Donne, wanted to discuss some tricky passages with me. It was a rich cultural experience, marred only by my spotting of the lady in black pointing us out to a burly plainclothes man as we were leaving the hotel one evening. I told Dick that it looked like we were being followed, but he said not to worry because it was ordinary for Russians to keep an eye on foreigners.

We took the train to Tallinn and on November 2 checked into a non-descript hotel, again the designated residence for foreigners. The room was rather long and narrow, with a sofa and chair at one end and two single beds at right angles at the other. I immediately noticed two strange features of the room. The sofa and table were separated from the bedroom area by a curtain, but the curtain rod did not have a curtain. And the little knob on the door lock did not work, so the room could not be locked from the inside. Again Dick reassured me that there was nothing to worry about, and we made ourselves at home, setting Dick's radio on the coffee table so that we could follow the buildup to the elections in the U.S. We had more vodka and caviar and, after smoking some grass, stowed it away in the brief case, which we put in the closet. We made love in my bed and then slept separately because the beds were so narrow.

The Old Town of Tallinn was indeed charming and beautiful, and the food was good. We made a reservation for 8:00 p.m. on November 4 at what the guide book said was the best restaurant in Tallinn. On both our second and third evenings we went to a Russian bath across from the hotel and then had a drink at the hotel bar. On the second night we made love and then, because the Russian bath was a bit enervating, had a nap before going to dinner. On the third night we followed the bath and drink with a brief listen to the news to find out if Eugene McCarthy would throw his support to Hubert Humphrey on November 4, the eve of the election.

We were just getting undressed in my bed for making love when there was a great racket at the door, with people shouting orders that I didn't understand but Dick did; he later told me that they were saying "Get that door open." "Quick, open that door." Dick leapt out of bed, hiding his erection with a pillow, as four men burst into the room, one of them with a flashing camera. I stayed in bed with my under shorts on until I was ordered to get up. I soon made out that they were the manager, a bellman, a translator who was also wielding the camera, and a man in a long black overcoat whose Moscow accent Dick construed and identified and who turned out to be a member of the KGB. Through the translator, they ordered us to move to the sitting room area while they did the "protocol of the room," which meant a thorough inspection of the bed. They found a tube of KY lubricant and a handkerchief that they suspected was stained with cum. As they ordered us to get dressed, I managed to say "All of this because you were sitting on the side of my bed discussing whether or not McCarthy would throw his support to Humphrey"—telling Dick the line I was going to take. They ordered us to be silent and led us to a jeep-like vehicle that took us to the "medical expert." He ordered us to remove our pants and under pants and proceeded to inspect our ass holes and penises for evidence of cum. Had they burst into the room ten minutes later, he would have found some, but because they were premature, he didn't.

We were then driven to the police station, where we were separated, Dick being interrogated in Russian and me in English via the translator. They asked me when I had met Dick, how I had got to Oxford, why I was visiting Dick in Leningrad, and wasn't I having sexual relations with him. To the last question I said no, that I was sitting on the bed to discuss whether or not McCarthy would throw his support to Humphrey.

It was close to midnight when they told us we could go back to our hotel because we were too smart to try to escape, and that they would let us know the disposition of our case the following day. We walked back to the hotel, almost afraid to speak because they might have bugged our asses. Back in the room, Dick burned in the ashtray the book of addresses of people he had met in Russia and flushed the ashes, along with the grass, down the toilet. I burned the little diary I had been keeping and threw those ashes down the toilet. We wondered in a whisper, because we thought the room was bugged, why they hadn't searched the closet, and speculated that they were too preoccupied with sex to bother about other issues. We tried to go to sleep, but I was literally shaking with fear so I couldn't sleep. I knew eight years in prison was the standard sentence, that I would be the death of my parents who could not bear the shame of their son's imprisonment and its being written up in the papers, that my academic career would come to an end, and that I could not stand the thought of being in a prison where I did not speak the language of the other prisoners (Dick quipped in a whisper that he could at least practice his Russian), and that I would probably be raped. The night dragged on with the torture of these fears until finally the dawn broke.

Outside the room Dick said that he would phone the American embassy in Moscow, sticking with our version of what had happened. When he came back from the call, he told me that the embassy would send a lawyer to defend us in the trial and that, in the mean time, they would see what they could do. After another three hours of anxiety, Dick phoned the embassy again. The case had already reached the Ministry of Education, and they told the person that they were going to give us the benefit of an amnesty because it was the fiftieth anniversary of the revolution, that I was to be deported to Finland, and that Dick could remain in Leningrad if he wished.

It was pretty clear to us that they did not have the evidence they needed because they had bungled the break in and that the amnesty issue was a sham. I can hardly find words for the profound relief we felt as we awaited the return of the four men who had broken in the room. They came to the lobby of the hotel about 3:00 p.m., the KGB man in black obviously angry that we had escaped his clutches. They announced, because of the amnesty, we were to be taken under guard back to Leningrad, that I was to be deported under armed guard to Helsinki, and that Dick could stay as a student if he wished. We boarded the train shortly after this encounter. We separated in Leningrad, and I was taken to the train for Helsinki by a policeman who accompanied me on the evening train but got off when we reached the border.

I bought another plane ticket to London, and I stayed in London with a friend from Stanford who was there for a short vacation and whose phone number Dick had. Dick was told by the policeman who accompanied him to the student residence that he was free to stay unless he managed to commit another crime, in which case a man in a black coat would seize him. He was too frightened to stay, so he took a toothbrush and passport on a plane to Moscow where he made his way to the American Embassy. There he was questioned almost as ruthlessly by the military police as he had been in Tallinn by the KGB agent. But he stuck to our story, and they said that they would try to get him a ticket to London. He was afraid that he would be stopped at the gate, so he almost kissed the floor of the British Airways plane when he got aboard. When he got to London he phoned our mutual friend and got directions to the house where he was staying.

When we met, Dick was furious. He unfairly claimed that I had ruined his career, that he would never again be able to go to Russia. In a calmer mood, he speculated about possible reasons for the KGB singling us out. Perhaps, given his West Point background, he would return to the military where he could be blackmailed into revealing state secrets. Perhaps they just wanted to embarrass young Americans in the press. Perhaps they had no particular reason, but were just following up on our peculiar behavior in the Astoria, where he failed to return the key to the lady in black each night. We will never know.

In fact, when Dick got a job at Colgate several years later after teaching at Austin, the first thing they asked him to do was lead a study group to Moscow. He thought the axe would fall on him when he applied for a visa, but he and his students got their visas with no difficulty, and he has returned to Russia many times since. Probably the Russians, in a pre-computer age, were just incompetent in keeping track of people they despised or wanted to use. We patched up our relationship before Dick returned to the States and I returned to Harlaxton Manor, and we have remained close friends, though not lovers, ever since.

Dick had met a Russian man with whom he fell in love, and I had met, at the Manor, Marty Cogan, with whom I had fallen in love.

Stanford, California

Marty was a junior at Stanford, a brilliant young scientist and doctor in the making. I knew it was dangerous to have an affair with a student, but my experience in Russia had left me feeling that nothing mattered when compared to a Russian prison, indeed that nothing mattered at all except to go on living rather than commit suicide. Marty was a happy accident. In a course on Jacobean drama, we encountered incestuous relationships in the plays, and Marty, walking to lunch one day, said that he could not understand those relationships or homosexual ones. Somewhat out of the blue, but I didn't make anything of it until I got back to Stanford, became a Resident Fellow in a four-class dorm, and had my own cottage adjoining the dorm. Marty visited me on several occasions, and once he took me for a ride on his motorcycle so I had to embrace him from behind. I eventually told him I was in love with him, and he simply replied that he wasn't in love with me.

Marty had three gorgeous friends, with one of whom, it turned out, he was in love. He had the loan for a weekend of a beautiful house near the ocean in Monterey, right next store to Kim Novak's on the Seventeen Mile Drive. So I picked up Marty, Peter, Dan, and Jim and drove to Monterey, stopping on the way to gather supplies, including a hefty amount of food, wine, and gin for martinis. We had drinks before a sumptuous dinner, and during the meal, Marty, feeling drunk, said he was going to bed. I was booked to share the room with him and, when we had finished dinner and washed the dishes, I went to bed. Marty had been sick, and I petted his head, and went into my bed. He suddenly sat up on the side of the bed and said that, after all, he was in love with me. I got in his bed and we kissed and had simple sex before falling asleep.

The next day he was silent, but we did hold hands secretly as I drove us home, The following day he came to my cottage and announced that it was all a mistake, that he wasn't in love with me, and that we shouldn't make love again. We took a long walk, during which he told me that he was in love with Peter, but that Peter was not returning his love. When we got back to the cottage, I kissed and embraced him. When I felt he was getting hard, I took down his pants, slipped off his underwear, and sucked him off. Marty was a very sexy person, so that became the way we dealt with each other until I got the courage to strip him and fuck him. He liked that even more than being sucked off, so we had a rich relationship.

Marty did not go home to Los Angeles during the summer vacation because of work he was doing in a chemistry lab, but I did persuade him to accompany me to Ashland, Oregon for the Shakespeare Festival, and we had a grand time, eating well, going to good plays and making love in our spare time. During the Autumn quarter, Marty invited me down to Los Angeles to meet his mother and go to the Rose Bowl in which Stanford was playing. We stayed in a hotel, and one night, as we were getting ready for bed, Marty said that he did love me more than anyone but his mother, and that he was in love with me. My heart leapt.

Palo Alto, California

At the end of the year, I resigned as a Resident Fellow and moved into a rental house in Palo Alto. The four young men helped me move. Marty was off to medical school at Harvard, but we kept in touch and I visited him the following summer in Cambridge. We took a drive through the Blue Ridge Mountains of Virginia and visited a friend and former colleague of mine in Charlottesville. One night, as I slept and they watched the moon from the door of the barn, he seduced Marty. I could see the direction in which we were heading, and I did not want to stand between Marty and the life of several lovers that he wanted to lead. When he came back to Stanford for some post-doctoral work and eventually a job at the University of San Francisco, I introduced him to a friend in a gay bar, they hit it off, and Marty moved in with Jack. I regretted that introduction because Jack, terribly jealous of me, would not let Marty see me. Our lives parted for several years, then I read in the obituaries that Marty had died of AIDS. So our lives were parted forever.

Back in Palo Alto, the summer I moved into the rental house and Marty left for Cambridge, Dick Sylvester visited from the University of Texas at Austin with a handsome young man. Dick had contracted hepatitis, and spent most of the summer recuperating. Peter visited, and we reminisced about Marty. I asked him why he didn't love Marty in return, and he said the prospect of a gay life was too frightening. I decided to housesit in the autumn for a colleague and his wife who lived next door and were going off to England on a sabbatical. I invited Peter over for dinner, and I put on a Roberta Flack record in the hopes that Peter would ask me to dance, which he rather impulsively did. I could feel him getting hard when he suggested that we might make love, just once, if I was agreeable. We undressed on the couch, I kissed Peter all over his body, and finally sucked him off. He said I must never do that again and led me into the bedroom where he came again almost immediately when I played with him. So the irresistible Peter who would not give himself to Marty gave himself to me.

In the autumn of 1972, I did a directed reading on Renaissance poetry with a young Scottish graduate student, Ken. I later met him at a party that friends of his threw. He said he had fallen in love with me when I read aloud the love poems of Philip Sidney. He came home with me that night and we made love for the first of many times over the next four years. Our relationship was, for a long time, very good. We shared intellectual and academic interests, we loved the opera, ballet, and theater, and we both liked to eat. Ken was a marvelous cook, and we entertained colleagues and students to meals that made him and me proud. We traveled to Britain to work at the British Museum library together and enjoyed cheap Indian meals nearby. We even survived a move to an apartment when the owner of the house I had been renting decided to sell.

Then things began to go sour. Ken was not making progress on his dissertation, and he began to drink very heavily. In fits of rage he threw coffee cups at the ceiling. We were bored with our sexual life and began to make visits to the local baths. I fell in love with a senior student, and on one glorious night we made love. I made the mistake of telling Ken and he said that he would leave me if I ever did so again. It was kind of an empty threat, because he had no place to go, but I didn't want to hurt him even more.

So we decided to stick it out until his student visa expired in 1977, and Ken went back to Britain, both of us saving face with our friends. He is a wonderful correspondent, and we have kept in touch over the years. I have frequently visited him in London, where he has lived until recently with his English lover, John. They have now moved to the south of France where it is cheaper to live off Ken's pension from the Venezuelan Oil Company for whom he worked as London office manager for several years.

I had finally received tenure at Stanford in 1971, and that promotion improved my salary and my professional confidence. I had been going back to St. Louis during the Christmas and New Year holidays to visit my parents. My father died in 1970, and I made a special trip back to protect my mother from the vultures at the local funeral parlor who did, as I expected, try to shame her into buying an expensive casket and an extended viewing period: "You don't have to live here, but your mother does, and what will her friends and neighbors think if you skimp on the services we can provide." We settled on a cheap coffin and one day of viewing.

That year I attended what had become an annual holiday party in the basement of one or two of my high school friends. The party this year was at Vic Witte's, formerly one of my debate partners and now a lawyer working for the NLRB. All the women were grouped on one side of the room and all the men across from them. Out of the blue, and without prompting, Bob Breer stood up, marched to the center of the room, and began a tirade against gay people. "All those queers are sick, sick. They ought to be killed. If I wouldn't go to jail, I'd strangled them myself." Vic, obviously embarrassed, said "Come off it, Bob. Get off your soap box." Bob ignored him. "Those perverts fuck with our kids. They try to make them queer." I couldn't take it any more and stood up: "Well, Bob, you can start by strangling me. I'm queer, always have been." A hush fell over the room—of surprise, perhaps of hostility. Vic apologized as Bob slid into a chair and I walked upstairs, about to leave. "Why don't you bring your mom to dinner tomorrow? About 5 o'clock." They weren't all homophobes, or at least weren't willing to acknowledge it.

About the same time I began to sense the difficulty of being openly gay in the university environment. One night I was going to a film with a colleague in the department, who I thought was my good friend, and I rather impulsively told him I was gay. He almost stopped the car and said: "I wouldn't tell anyone else that. I've known people who have lost their job for being homosexual." I later learned that he was right; one of his dear friends had been fired at one of the University of California campuses despite having tenure and being a superb poet. I saw it closer up at Stanford when a classics professor was found to possess some indiscreet photographs and was fired . I felt the threat directly when I was asked to lead an alumni field trip to England and Scotland. I asked if I could bring my partner, Ken Budge, on the trip because his knowledge of Britain would be a great asset. The woman in charge of alumni ventures said that a homosexual couple would make the older alums very uncomfortable. I didn't go on the trip. In fairness, I have to admit that attitudes have changed over the years: two years ago a partner and I helped lead a Mediterranean cruise for alums.

Ken's departure, even though I wanted it, left me rather desolate and lonely. I had the good fortune to run into a former student who was ushering at a concert and working for the alumni association. I courted Mark and, after a while, succeeded, He was an aspiring ballet dancer and a very smart historian. We had some good times at Ashland, and I nursed him through a broken ankle. He introduced me to his parents, and we often took Sunday walks, hand in hand, in Menlo Park. Imagine my surprise when, one Sunday, at a concert at Stern Grove in San Francisco, he announced that he wanted to end our love relationship and become friends. I had no choice but to comply.

At a meeting in my apartment for a gay faculty and staff organization that a colleague and I were forming, I met Patrick and began to see him during my second stint as a resident fellow. The other important new love of my life was an advanced graduate student, Lowell, whom I met at a party given by some graduate students. He was just coming off a heart-breaking bust up with someone and said he was not in the best position mentally and emotionally to take on a new relationship. But he gave it a try.

When I moved out of the resident fellow's cottage in 1984 and was heading toward a house in Palo Alto on loan from a friend who was moving to Sweden temporarily, I asked Lowell to move in with me. He refused though he did spend a lot of time in that grand house. Patrick said he wanted a room because his housemates in Palo Alto were disbanding their households. He moved in, and he moved again when we had to give up the house in 1992 and finally take up residence in a house that I had bought in 1982 and had been renting out. Patrick and I remain housemates and very good friends. The relationship turns out to be the most important one in my life. Patrick cares for me when I am ill or am recovering from an operation on my back—a too frequent occurrence. Because he is an engineer at Stanford's linear accelerator, I don't understand what he does in any depth, but we have many things in common: love of travel, opera, plays, and the symphony.

Lowell and I had some good times at Ashland, on camping trips, and at a performance of *The Ring* in Seattle. He is an opera buff, and under his influence I began buying season tickets to the opera in San Francisco. But one night he told me that he was no longer in love, and that he wanted to find someone with a great deal of body hair. We remained friends, and he left for a job in Los Angeles after he finished his dissertation.

I have many interests that I haven't made much of in this memoir. My mother, a dear and undemanding woman, fell in St. Louis, severely damaging her back, and, with my assistance, made the flight to the Bay Area for an operation and rehabilitation. I finally got her into a retirement home nearby that could accommodate wheel chairs, and we spent Sundays playing cards, going to movies, or dining out. The only time she made an issue about my being gay was years ago in St. Louis when I told her that I loved men. She said that she would die of shame if her friends and neighbors knew, but that the world would be a boring place if everybody were the same. Her death in 1989 –she broke her pelvis when when she fell between her chair and the wheel chair and rapidly declined—was one of the saddest days of my live. Oddly enough, my father had also died of complications of breaking his pelvis when falling off a ladder.

I was interested in debate and public speaking when I was in high school, and our debate team won several state championships and placed third in the nationals. I thought about studying law, having the romantic image of Perry Mason in the courtroom as my model. I haven't been involved in politics in the sense of running for office, but I have been engaged politically since I was a boy and heard my father, that ardent Roosevelt democrat, complain about the bank's attempts to thwart the formation of a union.

Partly as a result of my father's experience, I have an abiding hostility to figures of authority. As an elected member of the Academic Senate at Stanford. I had a contentious relationship with the presidents and provosts I outlived. With my colleague John Manley of Political Science, I finally won a battle. We had been attacking Stanford's relationship with the Hoover Institution, clearly a right-wing think-tank that should not belong under the Stanford umbrella. Friends remember me chaining myself to the massive doors of Hoover Tower to prevent entry. It's a lovely myth that I would like to embrace, but it's simply not true. Our protests came in the form of letters to the campus paper and attacks in the Academic Senate to which I was regularly elected.

The problem came to a head in the fall of 1983 when Ed Meese negotiated with Hoover the placing of the Ronald Regan Library, Museum, and a Policy Center to be run by Hoover, on the foothills overlooking Stanford from the west. The proposed structure was enormous and would ensure that Stanford would be bound by the Hoover Tower in the east and the Library in the west. All of the former chairs of the Senate signed a letter making the modest proposal that the structure be scaled down or moved to the other side of the foothills and that the policy center not be run by Hoover. When the Senate debated the letter's proposal, Warren Christopher, then the president of the Board of Trustees, attended the meeting, promising he would only listen. Donald Kennedy, the president of the university at that time, acting in bad faith because he did not like the Meese proposal, supported it and attacked the letter. When it became clear that the debate was going against Meese and Regan, Christopher took the floor for twenty minutes, supporting the Meese project. But the letter was supported by a big majority of the Senate; not long after the debate Meese withdrew his proposal, and the entire structure was moved to southern California. Stanford was spared the Regan library, museum, and policy center—the only significant battle I won during my Stanford years.

I am of course interested in friends. I can honestly say that former lovers remain friends, and I have a range of friends that were never lovers. I am especially pleased to have two women friends that I made in the writing program who are a constant source of amusement. Susan Wyle, a straight woman, collects animals She has a rabbit, two song birds, a parrot named Blossom who is remarkably talkative, and a huge Newfoundland dog named Scout—all in a modest condominium. Ardel Thomas, a lesbian, is a fine athlete who has won medals in swimming and weightlifting in the gay Olympics. The three of us lunch together often and go to the opera and concerts in San Francisco. Patrick has taken an interest in opera, and we enjoy symphony concerts and opera in the city.

I have, of course, a professional interest in literature and drama, which I teach at Stanford and enjoy for its own sake. Hence my annual trips to Ashland, Oregon for the Shakespeare Festival and my service as a board member for the San Francisco Shakespeare Festival. I have published four books, three of which bear on Shakespeare. One of them is a literary biography of contemporary of Shakespeare. One is a study of Shakespeare's history plays and his philosophy of history, and another devotes a chapter to each of his plays, with a critical analysis of their meanings and theatrical strategies.

I love teaching, especially Shakespeare's poems and plays, and I teach a sophomore seminar on the subject every year. When I was giving my final lecture in a big course on Shakespeare, I decided I was going to go out with a bang. With the help of my teaching assistants, I got dressed up as Cleopatra, with a wig that made me look like an African bush woman and with stuffed stockings for boobs. I "died" with some of my favorite lines in Shakespeare and was carried out by my "servants," the TAs.

I have dabbled with golf and with the piano, but I never even reached par, and I certainly would not play the piano in public. So sex is not everything, but it does seem to punctuate my life at various moments with varying degrees of pleasure or pain.

Looking back on my life, I see a few things I would change. I would finish my dissertation before taking a job. I would not go through the terror of the Tallinn experience. I would have avoided tennis to spare my back. I would have Lowell prefer non-hairy men—a trivial matter compared with the other three. But all in all, I think I have been fortunate in love, friendship, and work, and that's about as much as a person can ask for, short of a happy immortality.

www.ingramcontent.com/pod-product-compliance
Lightning Source LLC
Chambersburg PA
CBHW021237280526
45784CB00005B/2137